CARNAVALIA!

AFRICAN-BRAZILIAN FOLKLORE AND CRAFTS

BY LIZA PAPI

RIZZOLI
NEW YORK

"Nanny, Nana! There are people
knocking at our door!"
"Mourrice, call your mom and dad!
Reisado is here!"

"The *Reisado* dancers are messengers from the *rei*—the king," Nanny said. "Tomorrow is *Natal*, Christmas Eve, Mourrice! They are here to wish us good luck for the New Year!" Nana said *Reisado* is the celebration that begins carnival season here in Brazil, every year between Christmas and Lent. Then she threw open the doors as a group in colorful costumes performed a dance to say hello.

"Come see, Mourrice. The man in front is the king! To one side of him is the master of ceremonies, who starts the dance with a whistle. On the other side is Mateus, another master who will get all these people to dance and sing for you. Together the king and the two masters represent *Três Reis*, the three kings who followed the star and visited the Christ child."

"But Nanny! Why is the king so shiny? Oooh— I want to touch him, but I'm afraid!"

"Don't be afraid, Mourrice. See the little mirrors in their costumes? The king and the masters all wear mirrors. They only visit the homes of good people. But if someone they meet should wish bad luck on them, the bad luck hits the mirrors and bounces back to that person."

"Come in everybody! Welcome to our home!" Nanny said.

We placed a big chair next to our Christmas tree as the king's throne. The performers came in, carrying a chest filled with masks and costumes. The musicians played maracas, an accordion, drums, wood flutes, and guitars, and sang a song praising Heaven to wish our family lots of good luck. "Listen—they're singing *Peça de Sala,* 'Objects in the Room.' It's a song about your family and the good fortune they wish for you and the neighborhood."

The *Reisado* performed many dances. In the dance called *Guerra,* or War, the master of ceremonies crossed swords with Mateus, and then with the king.

When they danced *Dança da Sorte,* the Luck Dance, they gave us a white handkerchief and Nanny put some money in it and gave it to them as a tribute.

Then they began dancing the *entremeios,* the small dances. With all of the costumes and masks in that chest, I bet they could go on dancing and improvising forever!

In *Zabelê* the dancer wore a mask of a *jacu* and imitated the sound and movements of the bird. Then someone dressed like a little *curiabá* monkey danced the *Curiabá.* There was even one dancer who pretended to be a fern in the *Folharal.* These dances were inspired by the plants and animals of African mythology.

"See that small frog who is coming now?" Nanny asked. "His name is *Cururu,* and he dances so well that you'll think he is a real frog!" We laughed and clapped.

Then three characters came out and everyone got quiet. "Ah, Mourrice," Nanny whispered. "Now it is time for the last dance. It is a sacred one called *A Alma, Diabo, e Anjo Miguel*—The Soul, Devil, and Angel Miguel. Watch carefully. The Devil tries to take the Soul to Hell, but then Angel Miguel comes and fights with him."

Suddenly—poof! There was an explosion and a flash of light in our living room! And poof! The Devil disappeared.

"Look, Mourrice, Angel Miguel has saved the Soul from the Devil!"

As we said good-bye to the performers, Nanny told me we would see them at *Três Reis Magos* and then at Carnival in February. "Just wait, Mourrice!" she said. "Soon you'll see *Frevo, Congo, Moçambique, Maracatú,* and more interesting characters than you ever imagined! Tomorrow, I'll take you to see the performance *Bumba Meu Boi,* or Jump My Cow!"

In Jump My Cow some of the dancers wore cow, bull, horse, and dog costumes. Nanny explained that the cows and dogs were from the nativity scene and that the little donkey that carried Mary to the manger was represented by the horse.

"But, dear one, to understand Jump My Cow you must also know that the Portuguese brought the Africans to Brazil as slaves when they colonized this country. This dance has meanings from both the African and Catholic faiths—the animals have double meanings. The Portuguese believe the cow is important because it was nearest to the Christ child in the nativity and shared its warmth and milk with the baby Jesus. To African-Brazilians, cows represent protection because they provide milk and good luck; bulls or oxen symbolize fertility and power.

"Owning a cow means having power, Mourrice. Jump My Cow! is a play about who has power in Brazilian society and who doesn't," Nanny said.

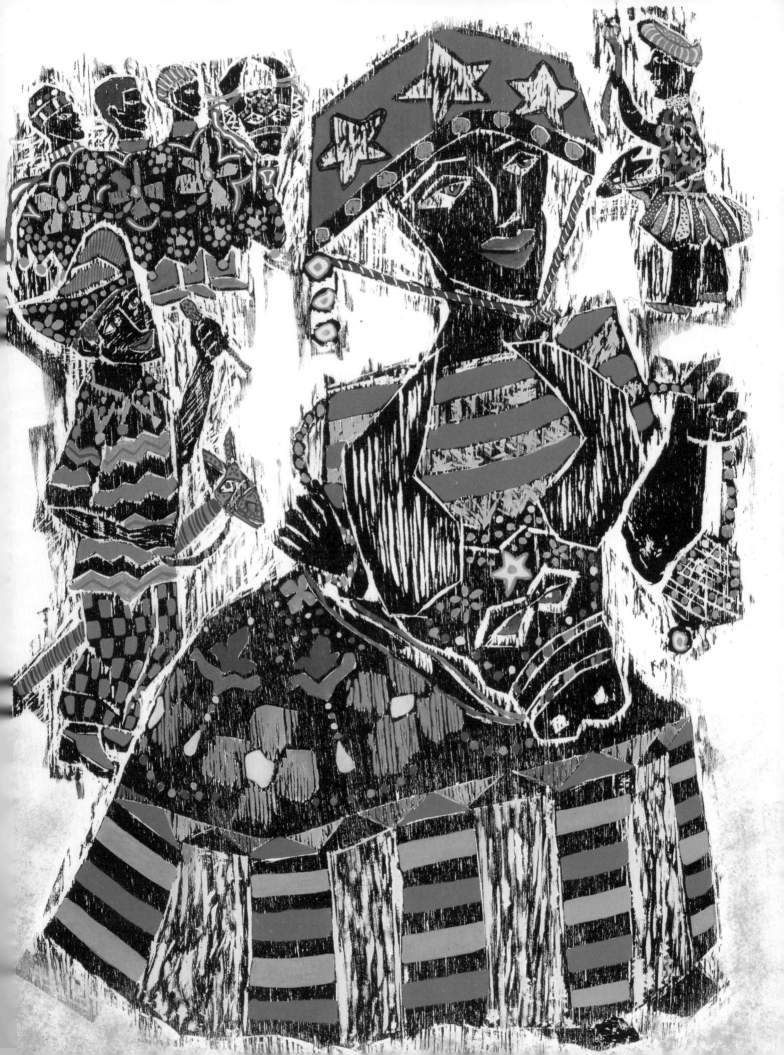

At the beginning of the dance the characters and musicians make a circle. One person plays a cow, and another man pretends to take the animal from the Portuguese farmer. A foreman helps him do this, and they bring the cow inside the circle. Everyone sings and dances around the circle, swinging their bodies to the rhythm of the rattles and drums. The characters tell jokes and make up funny conversations.

Suddenly the cow—who wasn't made for dancing—falls on the floor and dies. The men try everything to revive the animal. Nothing! They call upon an Indian with mystical powers and he brings the cow back to life. Now the animal belongs to everybody—the man, the foreman, and the Indian—not just the farmer. Everyone is happy. They clap their hands and yell, *"Bumba Meu Boi, Bumba Meu Boi!*—Jump My Cow, Jump My Cow!"

Nanny said this was her favorite performance because it involves all the races of Brazil—white, black, Indian, mulatto, *caboclo,* and *cafuzo.* "Plays like Jump My Cow! are one way for African- and native Brazilians to say that everyone should share the power in our country."

Nanny knows a lot about the folklore of Brazil. She learned it from her mother— who was Mom's nanny—and from her grand- mother, who was a slave for a rich Portuguese family in northern Brazil.

On *Três Reis Magos*, the Three Kings celebration on the sixth of January, we saw the *Reisado* dances and Jump My Cow performance again. I knew it would be only one more month until the big carnival in February. I couldn't wait! Imagine—four days of incredible parties! Nanny helped me make a different costume to wear on each day. When the first morning of Carnival came, I was awake and dressed in a minute's time!

Nanny and I walked to the parade and saw kids with big flags decorated with birds. "These flags will open the parade!" she said.

"I want to make a flag—full of birds, too."

"Use the birds that live in our own environment, Mourrice. In northeast Brazil we have *andorinha*—swallows—toucans, and wild black vultures. Or you could decorate your flag with the Brazilian flowers that remind you of spring."

After the group with the flags marched past us, I heard a drum rhythm that shook me inside out. Then someone in the crowd yelled, "Look! There's the *Frevo! Frevo* is coming!"

"It is the *Frevo*, Mourrice!" cried Nanny. "*Frevo* is the most exciting music and dance I ever saw. This dance is the soul of Carnival."

She took me by the hand to see that crazy dance
I'll never forget. The people were frantic, dancing wildly.
Some of them seemed completely out of their minds.
"*Frevo* comes from the Portuguese word *fervo,* which means
'boiling,' " Nanny said. "Watch, Mourrice, you dance *Frevo*
with one hand holding the umbrella. If you don't have
good balance, then forget it! You can fall right down."

I couldn't stop myself from dancing! It was so much
fun dancing *Frevo* in the street with everyone in the town.
People wore every kind of costume and we sang:

Se esta rua
se esta rua fosse minha,
eu mandava
eu mandava ladrilhar
com pedrinhas
com pedrinhas de brilhantes
para o meu amor passar.

If this street
if this street were mine
I would ask
I would ask to pave it
with many brilliant
with many brilliant diamonds
for when my love passes by.

The second day of
Carnival, I woke up and—
Oooh!—my muscles were
sore from the *Frevo*. I put
on my animal costume
and went to the garden to
wait for Nanny. While I
was there I saw my friend
Carlls Henry.

"Mourrice, guess what?
I just saw the scariest
mágico in the whole world
at the church square!" he
said. "You won't believe
that wizard!".

"Aw, Carlls Henry,
you are telling me a story!"

"No, dear, he's telling
you about the *Congo*
performance," Nanny said.
"It is about a king and
queen from the Congo,
in West Africa."

"And there's *mágico*—
a wizard—too?"

"Yes. Come on!"

In *Congo,* the royal family was made up of a king, queen, many princesses, and one prince. Many people escorted them: maids of honor carried a canopy to protect the royal family from the sun, which can be incredibly hot in Africa and Brazil; a captain, a foreman, and warriors marched on either side of the canopy to protect the royal family from their enemies.

And, of course, there was the wizard.

In a brief ceremony, the warriors gave the king and queen beautiful crowns glimmering with stones, golden flowers, and small mirrors. Then other dancers, playing enemy warriors, arrived on the scene.

The king's men fought with their wooden swords, but in spite of their courage, the enemy killed the prince.

Oh!—everyone was shocked and sad. The queen ordered the wizard to bring the prince back to life. If he couldn't, she said, she'd have him put to death, too!

The wizard was so scared by the queen's threats, he jumped up and pulled together all of his belongings: magical instruments, tobacco, and many dangerous snakes. He ran next to the prince's body, sang a beautiful African funeral song, and waved herbs over the body.

Then a miracle happened. The prince started moving— he woke up from the dead! The whole court rejoiced and sang another African song. The king promised the princess to the wizard to marry as his reward.

"See, Mourrice," Nanny said, "the powers of nature— her plants, herbs, and animals—can cure us. Today we dance *Congo* in honor of the patron saint of the African-Brazilians, Saint Benedito, who watches over us."

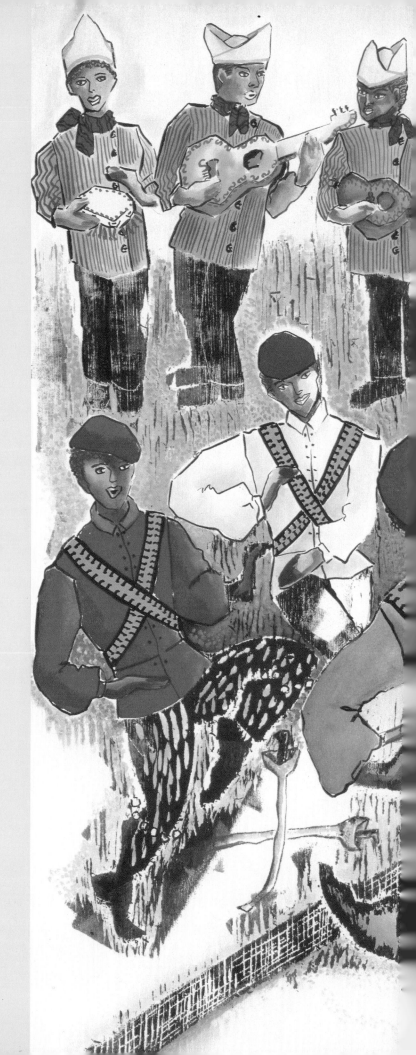

On the third day of Carnival we went to Carlls Henry's home, a big farm just outside of town. When Carnival dances weren't held at the church square, they happened here.

Carlls Henry wore this incredible *Moçambique* costume, with a small cap with ribbons, straight-pants, and bells around his knees. When he moved he made such a noise! I helped him place wood sticks on the floor in crosses for the dance, which represent swords from the battle between the Portuguese and the Africans.

"Nanny, I want to make a costume like that so I can jingle when I walk, too!"

"Ah—

Mourrice—*Moçambique* is not just for making noise. We dance it in honor of the Queen Njinga Nbandi of Angola, who dedicated her life to keeping her people from being sold into slavery. Her warriors fought many brave battles against the Portuguese slave hunters.

We dance *Moçambique* in remembrance of her.

"We also dance it for Saint Benedito, who protects the poor people of Brazil," Nana said.

Moçambique had a fast rhythm. Its music came from guitars and small drums, plus the noise of the bells on the dancers' pants and the sounds of the wood slapsticks. The dancers showed their agility and balance by dancing from one stick to the next. All the while, the bells on their legs jingled to the beat of the percussion band and we sang:

Vamos cantar,
Pedindo a Deus que abençoe
Nosso lar e nossos amigos
vou me despedir.
Queira aceitar meu aperto de mão.
Quantas histórias deixo na memória
Para a tristeza deixo o meu abraço,
E para a vitória meu coração.

Let's sing,
Asking God to bless
Our home and our friends.
I'm going to say good-bye.
Please accept my hand.
Many stories I leave behind with my good-bye.
For the sadness I leave my warm hug,
And for the victories I leave my heart.

On the last day of Carnival, Nanny dressed me as a prince for the most important African king and queen crowning, *Maracatú!*

From the time the Portuguese first brought slaves to Brazil in the sixteenth century until the end of slavery— 350 years later, in 1888—*Maracatú* was a solemn event. Some of the enslaved people had been kings in their African homelands and, even though they were in Brazil, the other slaves knew who among them were their *real* kings. They honored these men with this crowning and dance. Maracatú recognizes that some of the ancestors of the African-Brazilians were once kings.

The churchyard was decorated with palm trees and paper lanterns. Ribbons, confetti, and streamers filled the air, making designs in the sky as the crowd escorted the king and queen to their beautiful red velvet and gold thrones. The queen held a banner with a small *calunga* doll on top, an African symbol of hope and luck.

Then all the people who gathered in the churchyard danced for them.

Soon, everyone from the carnival groups—*Reisado,* Jump My Cow, *Frevo, Congo,* and *Moçambique*—joined us.

What a party! It was incredible—just incredible!

Northeastern Brazil, where this story takes place, is a region with exotic beaches and warm, dry weather. There are palm, coconut, and caraúba trees, and the crops include sugarcane, tobacco, and cotton. Because of centuries of interracial marriages, this part of Brazil has a unique mix of African, European, and native cultures—with some influences from Holland and Spain, brought by colonists from those countries. Brazil is the only country in South America where the people speak Portuguese.

In 1500, Portuguese explorer Pedro Álvares Cabral and twelve hundred men landed on the east coast of South America, at what is now Porto Seguro. They named Brazil after a redwood tree that grew in abundance there. In 1536, King João III of Portugal declared Brazil its colony, after which the Portuguese Jesuit missionaries forced the native Brazilians to convert to Catholicism and become slaves. As a result, many Indians retreated into the jungle and shied away from contact with whites. Beginning in 1538, the Portuguese brought Africans to Brazil as slaves. They captured these people in Angola, the Congo, and Mozambique. Princess Isabel of Portugal abolished slavery in Brazil on May 13, 1888.

Today, many African-Brazilians hold on to their African folklore and traditions. For example, even though the Jesuits forced the enslaved Africans to become Catholic, the Africans continued to worship their own gods by renaming them after Catholic saints. So, a saint may have both Catholic and African associations, and the religions are thus intertwined. African culture is shared by most people in Brazil—probably because many of the slaves worked as nannies for Portuguese children. African-Brazilian nannies had a unique place in society, since many were accepted as members of the white families and spent hours telling the children stories about Africa and their culture. Like Mourrice and Nana, children and their nannies developed deep, loving relationships, a fact that has done much to spread understanding between these two races in Brazil.

Carnivals rule Brazilian streets from Christmas to Easter. This is a time of street performances, merrymaking, and feasting that blends themes from the Roman Catholic faith, African and native heritage, and Brazilian history into a variety of public celebrations, including *Reisado*, Jump My Cow, *Frevo, Congo, Moçambique,* and *Maracatú.*

The largest of all Brazilian carnivals happens in the middle of February or early March, during the four days before Ash Wednesday. Ash Wednesday is a Catholic holiday that begins the observance of Lent, the weeks of solemn preparation for Easter. This carnival is the last celebration before Lent. Forty days later, people hold a ball on Hallelujah Saturday to celebrate Easter and the resurrection of Christ.

CARNIVAL CRAFTS

The crafts in this section were inspired by the performances and characters of African-Brazilian carnivals. The projects are designed for children age seven and up, but some crafts will require the help and supervision of an adult. They can be made from common, inexpensive or recycled materials.

WHAT YOU WILL NEED

Balloons	Newspaper	Ribbons
Beads	Nontoxic glue	Sandpaper
Colorful craft paper	Nontoxic paints,	Scissors
Fabric remnants	(such as tempera,	Sequins
Felt	poster, or acrylic)	Wheat paste (below)
Mixing bowls	Paint brushes	Wood sticks

RECIPE FOR WHEAT PASTE

One cup of wheat flour
Two cups of water

Mix the flour and water in a pot. With a parent's or teacher's help, bring the mixture to a boil for two or three minutes. Allow to cool before using.

REISADO HAT

The king of *Reisado* has a big hat shaped like the main church in town and richly decorated with mirrors, stones, and ribbons. He also wears a gold satin cape and a satin shirt decorated with mirrors, and he carries a scepter and a long wood sword. The two masters' hats are similar to the king's, except they are not as fancy and are sometimes decorated with paper flowers and colorful ribbons.

YOU WILL NEED

1. Scissors
2. Craft paper
3. Nontoxic glue
4. Nontoxic paint
5. Brushes
6. Sequins, beads, and ribbons

WHAT TO DO

1. Cut a 35 x 35-inch–square piece of paper.

2. Fold the paper in fourths. Open. Then fold it diagonally, from corner A to corner B. Open. Fold the paper diagonally again, from corner D to corner C. Open (diagram 1).

3. Fold the paper in half, from corner D to corner C, making a triangle shape (diagram 2).

4. Tuck corner A inside to corner C. Do the same to corner B, folding it inside to C and making a square, as shown (diagram 3).

5. Fold the paper diagonally in quarters as shown in diagram 4.

6. Tuck the four outer corners, marked E and H in front, and J and K in back (diagram 5), into the inside. This will make four triangular flaps: L and M in front, and N and O in back (diagram 6).

7. Fold flaps L and M into the center of one side of the paper (diagram 6).

8. Fold flaps N and O into the center of the opposite side of the paper (diagram 7).

9. Fold C up in front and in back (diagram 8).

10. Flatten corner I down to open the hat (diagram 9).

11. Glue the flaps to the cup of the hat.

12. Paint the front of the hat with your favorite style of church architecture.

13. Decorate with beads and big silver sequins, which have the same effect as the mirrors.

14. Attach colored ribbons to both sides of the hat.

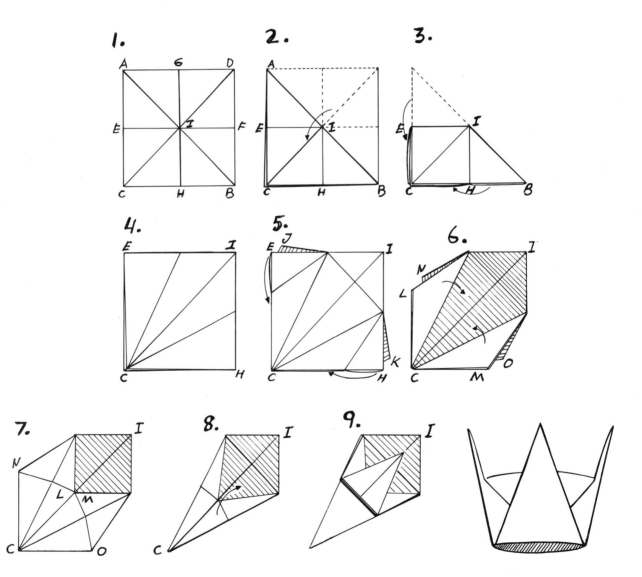

THE CANGACEIRO HAT

This half-moon-shaped hat is very popular in northern Brazil, where it became the characteristic costume of the *cangaceiro*, or cowboy. One of the most famous cowboys from that area was Lampião, the inspiration for movie romances and comic strips at the early part of this century. Lampião's leather hat was ornately decorated with Moses stars, a symbol of the northeastern Brazilian cowboys. It is worn by a number of the performers and musicians of Carnival, including *Reisado*, *Congo*, and *Moçambique*.

WHAT YOU NEED

1. Paper and pencil
2. Scissors
3. Nontoxic glue
4. Black ribbon
5. Solid-color felt:
   Three pieces 7¼ x 6½ inches
   Two pieces 21 x 8 inches
6. Scraps of contrasting colors of felt
7. Colorful ribbons

WHAT TO DO

1. With a parent's or teacher's help, enlarge patterns 1 and 2 on a copier machine to the sizes indicated.

2. Fold one piece of 7¼ x 6½-inch felt in half, along the 7¼-inch side, as in diagram 1. Place pattern 1 on the fold and cut out its shape.

3. Cut the other two pieces of 7¼ x 6½-inch felt in the same way so that you end up with three triangles, like diagram 2.

4. Glue the three triangles together, using black ribbon to cover the joints to make the beanie, as shown in diagrams 3 and 4.

5. Glue black ribbon around the bottom of the beanie to finish it. See diagram 5.

6. Fold one piece of 21 x 8-inch felt in half, along the 21-inch side, as in diagram 6. Place pattern 2 on the fold and cut out its shape.

7. Repeat this process on the other piece of 21 x 8-inch felt so that you end up with two half-moon shapes, such as diagram 7.

8. Glue the black ribbon around the edges of the half-moon shapes.

9. Glue the half-moon shapes to the front and back of the beanie. Glue black ribbon around the edges of the beanie and the half-moon brim that touch to hold those parts together, as shown in diagram 8.

10. Tie colorful ribbons through the holes at the sides to hold the front and back of the hat together.

11. Cut Moses stars and flower designs out of contrasting felt. Glue them on the front of the hat. See pattern below.

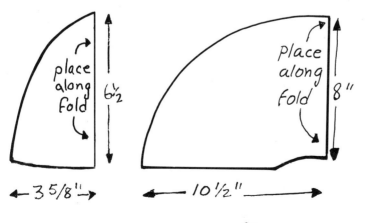

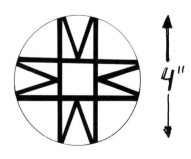

moses star

36

1.

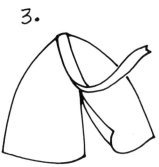

6½"

3 5/8"

2.

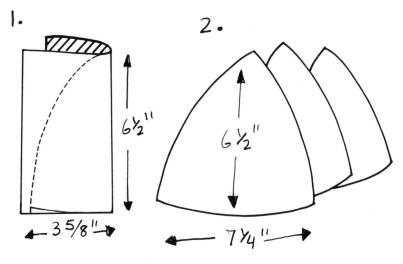

6½"

7¼"

3.

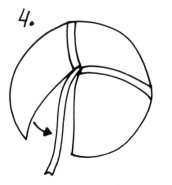

4.

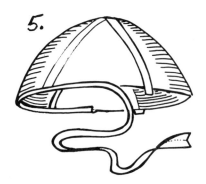

5.

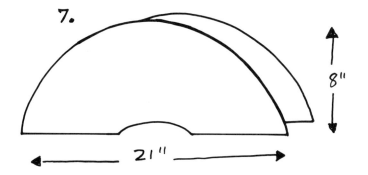

6.

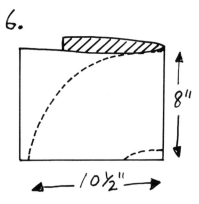

8"

10½"

7.

8"

21"

8.

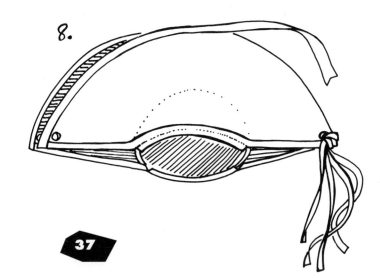

JUMP MY COW

THE COW

One of the most important characters in Jump My Cow is a black cow. It has a papier-mâché head decorated with ribbons and paper flowers, and a body that is made out of a colorful winding sheet that drapes over the dancer (or dancers) playing the cow.

YOU WILL NEED

1. Wheat paste
2. Newspapers
3. Balloon
4. Medium bowl
5. Cardboard or wire
6. Paint
7. Brushes
8. Ribbon

WHAT TO DO

1. Cover your work surface or table with newspaper to protect it.

2. Make the wheat paste mix, see page 32.

3. Cut the newspaper into strips half-an-inch wide.

4. Blow up the balloon to the size of a cow's head. Tie it.

5. Shred more newspaper into small pieces. In a medium bowl, mix this paper with some of the wheat paste until it feels like clay.

6. Apply a handful of this paper-and-wheat-paste clay to the balloon, as shown in diagram 1. Shape it into the cow's snout.

7. Place the half-inch strips into the paste until saturated. Remove excess paste by pulling the strip between your fingers.

8. Apply the saturated strips to the balloon, one by one, until the balloon is covered (diagram 2).

9. You will need to apply six to eight layers in order to make the head durable. Allow each layer to dry before applying the next.

10. Make ears and horns for your cow out of cardboard or wire. Make two half-moon shapes for the ears and two long, pointed shapes for the horns (diagram 3).

11. Attach the ears and horns to the sides of the cow's head. Secure them with the paste-saturated paper strips. Let dry.

12. Apply several layers of papier-mâché to make the ears and horns durable (diagram 4). Let the paste dry in between each layer.

13. When the mask is dry, use sandpaper to smooth the surface.

14. Paint the cow's head.*

15. Decorate with ribbons.

* Note: If you use water-soluble paints, you might ask an adult to help you apply a thin coat of varnish on the paint to protect it.

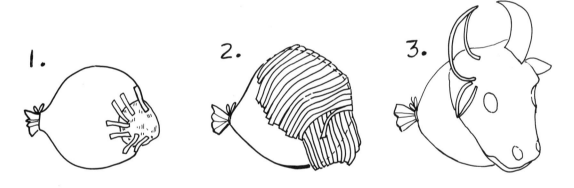

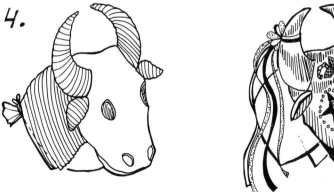

THE WINDING SHEET

The winding sheet, or *mortalha*, is the "body" of the cow. It is made of cotton fabric in a rectangular or half-moon shape — large enough to cover the dancer or dancers playing the cow.

YOU WILL NEED

1. Scissors
2. 2 yards of a solid-color fabric, and colorful scraps
3. Paper and pencil for sketches
4. Contrasting fabric or felt
5. Nontoxic glue
6. Nontoxic fabric paint
7. Brushes
8. Beads and buttons
9. Trim or lace

WHAT TO DO

1. Cut the solid-color fabric in a half-moon shape or rectangle to form a cape.

2. Make sketches of flowers or animals. Cut them out of contrasting fabric (or felt) and glue them to the cape.

3. Paint some details on the cape, and glue the beads and buttons.

4. Finish the edges of the cape with decorated trim or lace.

5. Cut long fabric strips and braid them to make the cow's tail.

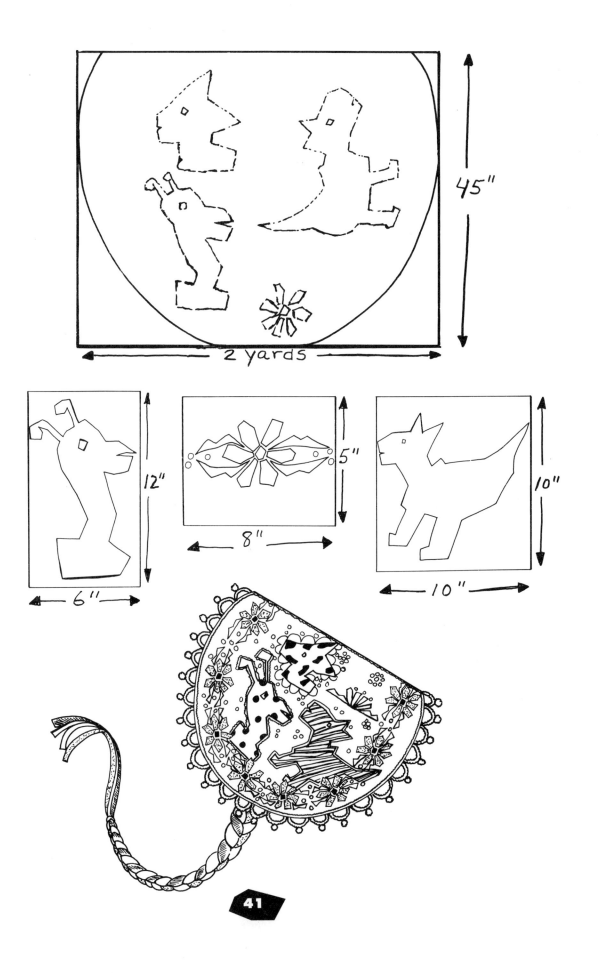

45"

2 yards

12"

6"

5"

8"

10"

10"

FLAGS

People carrying flags lead the parade to announce Carnival. The flags are decorated in many themes. Below you will find patterns for a flag featuring three birds from northeastern Brazil: the swallow, toucan, and black vulture. Or you can create your own designs featuring the flowers and birds that live in your area.

YOU WILL NEED

1. Scissors
2. A piece of fabric or canvas for the background of the flag, at least 20 x 30 inches
3. Chalk or soft pencil
4. Fabric of contrasting colors, such as felt, for appliqués of birds
5. Nontoxic glue
6. Two wooden sticks — one 24 inches long, one 48 inches long
7. Cord
8. Ribbons

WHAT TO DO

1. Cut the fabric for the flag. Trim the top and bottom corners, as shown.
2. With chalk or a soft pencil, sketch the shapes of the birds on the contrasting fabric.
3. Cut out the shapes. Lay them on the background to make a pleasing design.
4. Glue the bird shapes to the background.
5. Tie the two wood sticks together with a cord, making a cross. Tie the back of the flag to the sticks with a cord as shown.
6. Apply colorful triangle shapes to the bottom of the flag.
7. Wrap the sticks with ribbons.

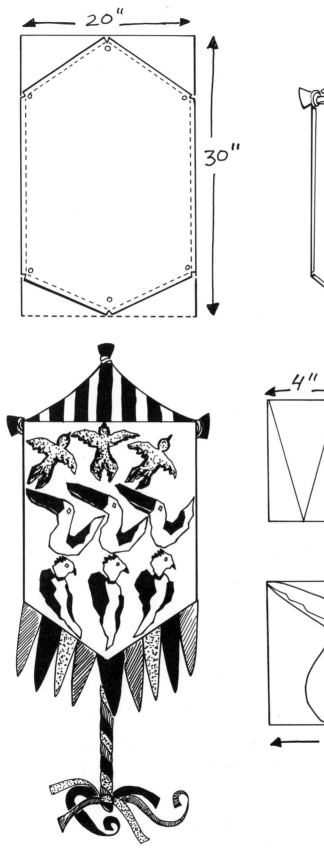

20"

30"

48"

24"

4"

7"

7"

7"

7"

7"

7"

7"

8"

8"

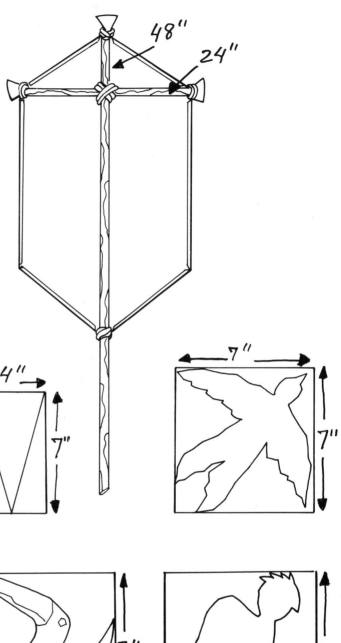

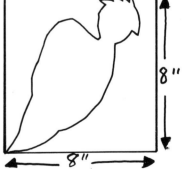

FREVO UMBRELLA

The umbrella used for *Frevo* is decorated with bright colors, flowers, geometric designs, and colorful ribbons.

YOU WILL NEED

1. Scissors
2. Craft paper in several colors
3. Pencil
4. Cardboard
5. Wood stick, about 30 inches long
6. Nontoxic glue
7. Ribbons

WHAT TO DO

1. Make a rectangle, 30 x 12 inches, out of colored craft paper.

2. Mark one-inch intervals along the top and bottom of the rectangle, along the 30-inch-long sides. See diagram 1.

3. Cut a cardboard circle, 5 inches in diameter, with a hole in the center. Attach it to the stick about 5 inches from the end and glue it in place with a paper stay, as shown in diagram 2. This will support the umbrella.

4. Cut flowers or geometric designs out of the colored paper.

5. Glue the flowers in place on the rectangle as in diagram 3. Let dry.

6. Fold the rectangle accordion-style along the one-inch marks (diagram 4). Then make small holes at one end of the folded paper and thread a ribbon through the holes.

7. Glue the two 12-inch sides to make a large tube (diagram 5). Let dry.

8. Tie the ribbon, gathering one end of the paper tube.

9. Place the umbrella on top of the stick. Tie it securely to the stick with the ribbon. Then tie the ribbon in a bow (diagram 6).

10. Decorate the wood stick by wrapping it with ribbons and tying ribbons to the handle.

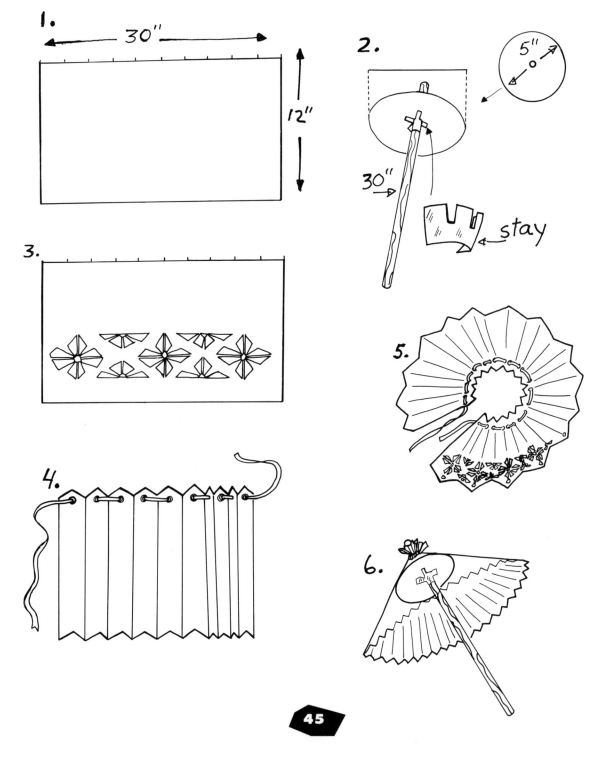

CONGO SNAKES

In African folklore, snakes are a symbol of danger and powerful magic. Their skin colors and patterns influence the decorative fabrics, clothing, ceramics, and crafts of Africans, and African-Brazilians. You can make four kinds of snakes from the story out of paper mâché.

1. **Rock Python** (Africa)—Pythons are among the largest snakes. Their skins have beautiful geometric designs in earth tones and black, white, and gray.

2. **Anaconda** (South America)—Anacondas measure as long as twenty-nine feet. Their skins have round designs in warm earth colors.

3. **Boa Constrictor** (northern Brazil)—Boa constrictors are from thirteen feet to forty-eight feet long. Most of them are black, cream, or white.

4. **Emerald Tree Boa** (northern Brazil and the West Coast of Africa)—A member of the constrictor family, this snake is emerald green with white geometric markings.

EMERALD TREE BOA

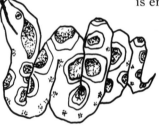

BOA CONSTRICTOR

YOU WILL NEED

1. Newspapers
2. Wheat paste
3. Medium bowl
4. Sandpaper
5. Nontoxic paint
6. Paint brushes

ROCK PYTHON

ANACONDA

WHAT TO DO

1. Cut the newspaper into strips no larger than one-half-inch wide.

2. Prepare the wheat paste, see page 32.

3. Shred more newspaper into small pieces. In a medium bowl, mix this paper with some of the wheat paste until it feels like clay. Shape this "clay" into a snake's body—you can coil it, or make it curvy.

4. Apply paste-saturated strips over the snake's clay body. Wipe the excess paste from the strips by pulling it between the fingers.

5. After you've done one layer of the paste-saturated strips, apply one layer of water-moistened paper. Then start again with the layers of paste-saturated paper. Apply the layers in different directions to make the snake's body stronger.

6. When thoroughly dry, sand the surface so it is smooth.

7. Paint the snake with white paint.

8. Decorate with the markings of one of the snakes listed above. See the full-color illustration of these snakes on pages 20 and 21 or decorate the snake with the markings of snakes that live in your area.*

* Note: If you use water-soluble paints, you might ask an adult to help you apply a thin coat of varnish on the paint to protect it.

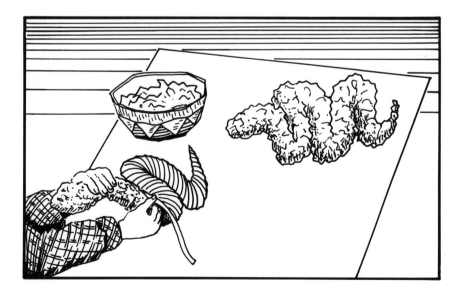

GLOSSARY

Ash Wednesday—The first day of Lent.

Caboclo—A person of mixed European and native Brazilian racial heritage.

Cafuzo—A person of mixed African and native Brazilian racial heritage.

Colonize—When a group of people settle in a new territory but remain bound to the government or customs of their mother country.

Easter—The Christian commemoration of the death and resurrection of Jesus Christ.

Folklore—Traditions, beliefs, and stories passed from one generation to the next in a culture, usually through the spoken word.

Jacu—A bird from Northeast Brazil, a member of the chicken family.

Jesuit—A follower of the Roman Catholic Society of Jesus founded by Saint Ignatius Loyola in 1534, devoted to missionary work and education.

Lampião—One of the most famous cowboys from northeastern Brazil, the inspiration for movie romances, comic strips, and folklore in Brazil.

Lent—The forty weekdays from Ash Wednesday to Easter. A solemn time of fasting and preparation observed in the Roman Catholic church.

Maraca—A rattle-like percussion instrument, sometimes made out of a gourd.

Missionary—A minister assigned by a religious organization to spread its faith to non-believers.

Mulatto—A person of mixed African and European racial heritage.

Mythology—A group of stories about the gods, heroes, or legends of a culture.

Natal—Christmas in Portuguese.

Nativity—The birth of Jesus Christ.

Queen Njinga Nbandi—The African Queen who lived in Angola in the early 1600s who fought to protect her people from Portuguese slave catchers.

Saint Benedito—The patron saint of African-Brazilians.

Três Reis Magos—The Three Kings celebration on the Sixth of January, known as *Epiphany* in the Catholic Church.

To Mourrice with love.

The many years of research required to write this book started with the help of my wonderful friend Celia Messias, director of the Lower East Side Arts Center, New York. I also thank my dance teacher, Ivy Epstein, who helped me understand the inner power of contemporary and native dance. I am grateful to singer Uyara and to the popular writers of northeastern Brazilian for their Cordel Literature, which reflects the integrity, originality, and courage of their people. And, since life in Brazil is so related to the environment, the Buddhist writings of Nichiren Daishonin helped me further understand this balance.

Special thanks to my editor Kimberly Harbour, whose openness and sensitivity helped me throughout the process of creating this book. And thanks to my special friends: Fernando Natalici, who helped me print the woodcuts; Professor Dr. George N. Preston, whose specialty is African-American and Brazilian art; cartoonist Nilson de Azevedo; and musicians David P. Appleby, Richard Di Donato, and Leonel Costa. Thanks to Carroll Davey of The New York Public Library for reviewing the manuscript and craft instructions.

Warm thanks to my family who gave me courage and helped me search for unique folklore material: to my son Mourrice, his father and my best friend Osni Omena, my mother Lair B. Papi, my sister Nariman B. Papi, my aunts Myra Papi de Guimaraens and Sonia Papi de Moraes, my cousins Vanessa Bronson and Dinah Papi de Guimaraens. I also thank my friend and Buddhist leader Janice Jacob, who is also a wonderful painter.

First published in the United States of America in 1994 by
RIZZOLI INTERNATIONAL PUBLICATIONS, INC.
300 Park Avenue South, New York NY 10010

Copyright © 1994 Rizzoli International Publications, Inc.
Illustrations Copyright © 1994 by Liza Papi

Library of Congress Cataloging-in-Publication Data

Papi, Liza.
    Carnavalia! : African-Brazilian folklore and crafts / by Liza Papi.
        p.   cm.
    ISBN 0-8478-1779-2
    1. Carnival—Brazil—Juvenile literature. 2. Blacks—Brazil—Social life and customs—Juvenile literature. 3. Arts, Brazilian-African influences—Juvenile literature. 4. Brazil—social life and customs—Juvenile literature. I. Title.
GT4233.A2P36   1994
394.2'5'0981—dc20   93-38451
                                                            CIP

Edited by Kimberly Harbour
Designed by Barbara Balch
Jacket Illustration by Liza Papi
Printed and bound in Hong Kong